GRADE
2

who   what   where

when   how

FLASH FORWARD READING

fact   opinion

Written by **Kerrie Baldwin**

Illustrations by **Dave Garbot**

Flash Kids™

Spark Publishing

Spark Publishing
A Division of Barnes & Noble
120 Fifth Avenue
New York, NY 10011
www.sparknotes.com

ISBN-13: 978-1-4114-0704-6
ISBN-10: 1-4114-0704-0

For more information, please visit *www.flashkidsbooks.com*
Please submit changes or report errors to *www.flashkidsbooks.com/errors*

Printed and bound in the United States

1 3 5 7 9 10 8 6 4 2

The Maya of Mexico

    Juan went on a special vacation last year. His family flew all the way to Mexico! That is where his grandparents live. Juan loved visiting them. Their house was pink and yellow. They told Juan about the *Maya*. The Maya were one of the first people in Mexico. Their homes and buildings were made of stone. The stone buildings are empty now. Only the ruins are left. Juan wanted to see the Maya ruins! The family took a bus to the jungle. It was very green and hot there. A guide took them up a big hill. Juan saw a whole stone city. The guide told them that the Maya built it themselves without any machines! Juan couldn't believe how much of the city was still standing. It must have been very beautiful.

Answer the questions below.

1. Where did Juan go on vacation? _____

2. Who took Juan's family to see the ruins? _____

3. What is the name of the people who lived there? _____

Dinosaur Daydream

Amanda doesn't watch a lot of television. But she likes shows about dinosaurs. She likes to see what dinosaurs looked like. Apatosaurus was tall. It had a very long neck. Tyrannosaurus rex was tall, too. It could stand on its back legs. It had very sharp teeth. Tyrannosaurus rex ate animals and other dinosaurs. Amanda's favorite dinosaur is Stegosaurus. It was a calm dinosaur. It ate plants. It had bony plates along its back. The plates helped Stegosaurus. They protected it from bigger dinosaurs. Amanda imagines riding on top of Stegosaurus. She could hold onto the plates. That would be so fun! Amanda wishes that dinosaurs were still around. They all died many, many years ago. No one is sure why. But Amanda can still daydream about them!

Read each question. Circle the right answer.

1. What is Amanda's favorite dinosaur?
   a. Apatosaurus
   b. Tyrannosaurus rex
   c. Stegosaurus

2. What did Stegosaurus eat?
   a. plants
   b. animals
   c. people

3. When did all the dinosaurs die?
   a. ten years ago
   b. yesterday
   c. many, many years ago

Rubber Report

What do bubblegum and the bottom of sneakers have in common? They stick to each other! But there's more. Did you know that they are both made of rubber? Rubber is stretchy and bouncy. It is a fun material used to make lots of things we use today. It wasn't invented in a lab. It is found in nature. Rubber comes from special trees. The rubber trees don't bend and stretch, though. The rubber is inside the trees. It is right under the bark. First it is a liquid called *latex*. You can scratch the bark and let the latex drip out. If you catch the latex in a cup, it will harden into solid rubber. The rubber doesn't want to turn back into latex. Rubber stays in its shape. It keeps cool, too. Rubber is good for tires. You don't want tires to melt or catch on fire!

Read each sentence. Circle *true* or *false*.

1. Rubber comes from the rubber fish.   true   false

2. Bubblegum is made of rubber.   true   false

3. Rubber keeps cool.   true   false

Making Meatballs

   "Ben! Come help make dinner!" Ben's mom is calling him. Ben walks into the kitchen. He sees pots on the stove. There is a box of pasta on the table. Tonight is pasta and meatballs. This is his favorite dinner. Ben doesn't mind helping. He will make the meatballs. First, he washes his hands. Then he takes meat and eggs from the refrigerator. Ben cracks open the eggshells. Then he mixes the eggs with the meat. Next, he adds breadcrumbs and spices. He squishes it all together with his hands. This is the best part! Then he rolls little pieces into balls. These are the meatballs. Now he needs to cook them in tomato sauce. Ben looks for the jar. It's not in the refrigerator. It's not in the cupboard. His mom lifts the lid off a pot. The sauce is inside. Mom always has everything ready!

Answer the questions below.

1. What is Ben's family eating for dinner? _____

2. Who is making the meatballs? _____

3. Where is the tomato sauce? _____

A Special Statue

Gavin opened the front door and ran to Dad. Gavin was jumping up and down. Dad stopped him. Was something wrong? He just wanted to tell Dad about the class trip. His class went to New York City that day. It was a beautiful and very busy place. Gavin had never seen that many people on the street. He rode a boat for the first time, too. It was a special boat called a ferry. The ferry took his class across the harbor. It looked like they were floating toward a woman. She kept getting taller and taller. This was the Statue of Liberty. It is one of the most famous statues in the world. His class went inside the statue, too. Gavin had so much fun!

Finish each sentence.

1. Gavin took a trip to New _____ City.

2. He rode a special boat called a _____.

3. The Statue of Liberty looked like a very tall _____.

A Kind of Compass

Sydney sits down on a rock. She drinks from her water bottle. Hiking makes her tired! Sydney and her older sister have been hiking all afternoon. But now it's getting late. They don't want to be lost in the dark. They must return to the tent by sunset. Sydney remembers that they need to hike north. Sydney's sister knows how to use a compass. The needle on the compass shows the direction. She finds north. Then they start hiking. Sydney sees the trees they passed earlier. This is the right direction. Soon they see the tent. And just in time! Sydney looks to the west. The sun is turning from orange to red. She watches it sink into the ground far away. The sun always sets in the west. Sydney knows that the sun is nature's compass.

Answer the questions below. Use the words in the word bank.

west   north   sunset

1. When must Sydney and her sister return to the tent? _____

2. Where do they need to hike? _____

3. Where does Sydney see the sunset? _____

Our One Sun

    Look at the sky on a clear night. Do you see stars? They look like tiny white lights. The stars appear small because they are far away. But you've seen one star look bigger and closer during the day! What is this special star? It's the sun! It's the star closest to earth. The sun is very bright. It gives a lot of light. The sun is very, very hot, too. Its heat reaches all the way to earth. The sun keeps earth warm enough for things to live here. But the sun isn't in the sky at night. Where does it go? The sun is still around. It is shining on the other side of earth. The sun didn't move, though. The earth turned instead!

Read each question. Circle the right answer.

1. What is the sun?
    a. a planet
    b. a star
    c. a lamp

2. From where does earth get its heat?
    a. sun
    b. Mars
    c. fire

3. What happens to the sun at night?
    a. It turns off.
    b. It puts on sunglasses.
    c. It shines on the other side of earth.

Super Summer Party

We are walking to the Sanfords' house. Today is their summer party. The Sanfords have it in their backyard every summer. They invite all the neighbors and their pets! We get closer to their house. I can see Buddy and Princess playing in the front yard. They see Sparky. They wag their tails. Sparky runs toward them. Then they all roll together in the green grass! We go to the backyard. My parents say hi to Mr. and Mrs. Sanford. They are cooking at the grill. The air smells like burgers. I hope I can have cheese on mine. But I want to see the other kids first. They are playing a game. Jesse rolls a big ball to Ashley. She kicks it and runs around the bases. It's kickball! I'm good at this sport. Ashley lets me join her team. I hope we'll win this year!

Draw a line from each group to what they're doing.

kids   cooking food

parents   rolling in grass

dogs   playing kickball

It's Stuck!

Brianna's grandmother was paying for the bags of food. Brianna saw a gumball machine outside the store. Her grandmother gave her a quarter. Brianna got a big red gumball. It tasted like a cherry! Brianna practiced blowing bubbles. But it was windy that day. The wind was blowing her hair around. Brianna's hair blew right onto a bubble. It was stuck! She couldn't pull the gum out of her hair. Would she have to cut it out? Her grandmother said not to worry. She would fix it when they got home. First, her grandmother put ice on the gum. That should have made the gum less sticky. It didn't work. Then Brianna remembered a trick she had heard. She took out a jar of peanut butter. The slimy stuff made the gum slide right out!

Read each sentence. Circle *true* or *false*.

1. It was a windy day.   true   false

2. Brianna put peanut butter on the gum first.   true   false

3. Brianna's grandmother cut out the gum.   true   false

Blue Bowling Ball

Weekends in the winter can be boring. Sometimes there isn't any snow to play in. Sometimes it's too cold to be outside. So Sean's family goes bowling! They drive to the bowling lanes. A lot of families are there. Sean sees a friend from school, too. Sean takes off his coat. Then he takes off his shoes. Does he want to wear the bowling shoes? Those shoes are smelly! Sean will bowl in his socks instead. Next, he chooses a bowling ball. He finds one that isn't too heavy. The ball is bright blue. That's his favorite color. Then Sean is ready to play. He rolls the ball down the lane. It hits eight pins. They fall down. There are two pins still standing. Sean rolls the ball again. It knocks over the two pins! Maybe the blue ball is good luck!

Finish each sentence.

1. Sean and his family go _____ in the winter.

2. First Sean takes off his _____.

3. The ball knocks down _____ pins in all.

Ice Cream Snow

A lot of kids eat ice cream in the summer. It cools them when the weather is hot. Some kids like ice cream in the winter, too. But if the ice cream truck isn't around and there isn't any ice cream in the freezer, where can you get ice cream? You can make it from snow! You don't even need an ice cream machine. First, measure a cup of milk and half a cup of sugar. Mix them in a big bowl. Then add only half a teaspoon of vanilla. Next, go outside and pick up some very white snow. Make sure it is clean! Run back inside and add a little snow to the bowl. Stir it. Keep adding snow until it looks like ice cream. Enjoy your treat! But hurry up. Ice cream still melts in the winter.

Answer the questions below. Use the words in the word bank.

snow   machine   vanilla

1. What don't you need to make ice cream? _____

2. What do you add half a teaspoon of? _____

3. What is the last thing you add to the mix? _____

Surprising Dad

Today is Dad's birthday. But Shelby won't wish him Happy Birthday yet. She is planning a surprise birthday party for him. She invited all the neighbors. They will come over at 4:00. There is a lot to do before then! First, Shelby walks to the store. She buys a bag of colored balloons. She buys cake mix and frosting, too. Mom is waiting at the front door. She says that Dad is taking a nap. Mom bakes the cake. Shelby blows up the balloons. She hides them in the closet. Then she decorates the birthday cake. It's almost 4:00! Shelby needs to get Dad out of the house. She has an idea. She wakes up Dad. She tells him that she's sick and wants ginger ale. Dad goes to the store. The neighbors come over. They have just enough time to hide. Dad will be so surprised when he returns!

What's the order? Draw a line to match each part of the story.

first   Shelby buys balloons.

second   Shelby tells Dad that she wants ginger ale.

third   Shelby decorates the cake.

Fighting Fires

Uncle Victor is very brave. He is a firefighter. His job is to stop fires. The fires aren't just in fireplaces. They are big fires. They burn houses and other buildings. Uncle Victor never knows when a fire will happen. He waits at the firehouse. Other firefighters are there, too. The bell could ring at any time, even during lunch. The bell means that they need to hurry to a fire. First Uncle Victor must put on a special jacket and hat. These clothes protect him from the fire. Then they all get in the fire truck. Their dog comes, too! They drive fast to the fire. It is burning a house. But the whole family got out. Uncle Victor sprays water at the house. The fire is stopped. The house is saved and no one is hurt. Uncle Victor's job is very important!

Read each question. Circle the right answer.

1. What is Uncle Victor's job?
  a. He starts fires.
  b. He plays with dogs.
  c. He stops fires.

2. Where does he wait?
  a. fireplace
  b. firehouse
  c. firefly

3. What does Victor do right after he hears the bell?
  a. He puts on his special jacket and hat.
  b. He finishes his lunch.
  c. He jumps in the fire truck.

Supper Salad

Danny learned about food at school today. He learned that vegetables are very important. Danny's mom says that he can make the vegetables for supper tonight. What can he make? A salad is easy. There are lots of vegetables in the garden. Danny goes outside. He picks some lettuce. He plucks some tomatoes. He pulls out some carrots. The vegetables look tasty, but they are very dirty. Danny must wash them first. Then he takes a knife. He carefully chops the vegetables into small pieces. He puts the pieces in a big bowl. He mixes them all up. The salad looks colorful. But something is missing. Danny opens the refrigerator. He takes a bottle of salad dressing. He pours a little on the salad. Now the vegetables are ready to be eaten.

Answer the questions below.

1. Where does Danny get the vegetables? _____

2. What does he use to chop them? _____

3. What is the last step? _____

Sleeping Like a Bear

Do you live near the woods? Have you ever seen a bear outside? You might! They are always looking for food. Bears eat fruit and berries in the summer. They eat acorns and nuts in the fall. Bears must fill their stomachs now. There won't be much food in the cold winter. Everything will be covered in snow. But the bears will be warm and safe. They sleep through the winter! First, a bear makes a bed called a den. The bear uses leaves and small branches. The den will keep the bear warm. Then the bear goes to sleep. It can sleep for months without eating. The winter passes. Spring is here! The air is warm and grass is growing. The bear wakes up to eat. It comes out of the den. But what are behind the bear? Two bear cubs are there!

What's the order? Write *1*, *2*, or *3* on the line.

_____ Bears sleep through the winter.

_____ Bears make dens from leaves and small branches.

_____ Bears and cubs wake up to eat.

Cutting for the Carnival

Tonight is the carnival. There will be so many rides and games. Lizzie wants to go, but she doesn't have any money. Maybe Lizzie can earn it. How can she work? She's too young for a real job. Her parents say that she can cut the grass. They will pay her a dollar. So Lizzie goes to the shed. She takes out the lawnmower. Lizzie pushes it and cuts the grass. Then she has an idea. She takes the garden hose and sprays the lawn. Water keeps the grass healthy. Lizzie's parents pay her two dollars instead! Lizzie would still like more money for the carnival. She asks the neighbors if they want their grass cut. They say yes. Lizzie cuts grass all afternoon. She waters it, too. Lizzie earns five dollars. She goes home and dinner is ready. Lizzie is very hungry from working all day, but she's not too tired for the carnival!

Finish each sentence.

1. Lizzie wants to go to the _____ tonight.

2. First she _____ the grass.

3. Lizzie is finished when _____ is ready.

Guys at the Game

Ethan won tickets to a baseball game. He and his dad love baseball. They are going to the game together. They put on baseball caps and ride the train. Soon they arrive at the baseball stadium. Ethan can't believe how big it is! They walk inside. There must be thousands of people here. They find their seats. Ethan and his dad are sitting close to home plate. These are great seats! Ethan can't wait for the game to begin. A man is selling hot dogs. Ethan's dad buys two for them. Ethan eats his hot dog right away. Then the baseball game begins. The Sliders are batting first. A player steps up to the plate. The ball zooms at him. He swings the bat. Crack! The ball flies high and far. It goes out of the stadium. It's a home run!

What's the order? Draw a line to match each part of the story.

first   The Sliders make a home run.

second   Ethan eats a hot dog.

third   Ethan and his dad find their seats.

Caught Kite

Marissa thinks that spring is the best season. Flowers are blooming. Birds are chirping. The weather is warm and very windy! Spring is the best time to fly a kite. Marissa and her brother Jared have contests. They see who can keep their kite in the air longer. She and Jared bring their kites to the big park. Marissa's kite is orange and red. Jared's kite is blue and green. They hold their kites and spools of string. The wind lifts the kites in the air. They turn the spools. The kites go higher. They look like small butterflies. Then the wind blows strong. Marissa's kite flies over to a tree. Her kite is caught around a branch! The wind blows strong again. It blows her kite free. Now she doesn't see Jared's kite. It is on the ground. Jared was too busy watching Marissa's kite. He didn't see that his kite was falling. Marissa wins the contest!

Answer the questions below.

1. What are Marissa and Jared flying? _____

2. Where does Marissa's kite get caught? _____

3. Who wins the contest? _____

Thunder and Lightning

    The sky is turning gray. Flash! Boom! What's that? Don't be afraid. It's just a thunderstorm. The rain will fall soon. The thunderstorm tells you that it's coming. First, you see the lightning. The whole sky may light up for a second. Look carefully. The lightning makes a wiggly line. It reaches from the clouds to the ground. Next, you will hear thunder. It is loud and can make you jump. The lightning and thunder will keep coming. They will get closer together. Do you see lightning and hear thunder at the same time? That is when the thunderstorm is right above you. Watch out for the rain! But don't run under a tree. Sometimes lightning hits a tall tree or building. Stay safe while you enjoy the show in the sky.

Answer the questions below. Use the words in the word bank.

> lightning   tree   thunder

1. What part of a thunderstorm comes first? _____

2. What part comes next? _____

3. What should you not stand under during a thunderstorm? _____

California Coast

Brian opens the mailbox. There's a postcard from Julia! She is Brian's best friend. Julia is on vacation for a month. She is in California right now. Brian learned about California in school. It is a big state. It is near the ocean, too. Julia had to fly west to get there. She writes about California in her postcard. She has seen mountains, forests, and deserts in California. Her family went hiking one day. Another day they saw some fruit farms. A lot of grapes are grown in California. Julia got to pick some! She feels very tired every night. She likes to go back to their hotel. Her bed is very soft. The hotel has a pool. Julia has gone swimming every morning. Today her family is walking to the beach instead. Julia is having a great time in California.

Read each question. Circle the right answer.

1. What is California?
   a. a big state near the ocean
   b. a small state in the middle of the country
   c. an island in the ocean

2. Where is Julia's family sleeping?
   a. a hotel
   b. a tent
   c. a boat

3. What is Julia doing next?
   a. picking grapes
   b. hiking in the forest
   c. walking to the beach

Rush, Rush!

Nicholas eats the last piece of potato. He's all done with dinner! He takes the dishes to the sink. It is Dad's turn to wash them. Nicholas looks at his watch. It says 6:45. Then he remembers that it's movie night. Once a week he can stay up late. But he has to start the movie by 7:00. Now he has only 15 minutes to get ready. Nicholas runs into the bathroom. He starts the shower. He jumps in. He washes himself as fast as he can. Next, he puts on his sleep clothes. He combs his hair. He is not done yet! Nicholas's room is a mess. He puts his toys in the big bin. Then he goes downstairs. Mom is making popcorn. It's movie time!

What's the order? Write *1*, *2*, or *3* on the line.

_____ Nicholas takes a shower.

_____ Mom makes popcorn.

_____ Nicholas's watch says 6:45.

Brushing and Flossing

Alexis finishes her sandwich. She eats a red apple for dessert. This was a good lunch. She will go outside to play in a few minutes. First, she needs to brush her teeth. Alexis brushes after every meal. That is three times a day. Brushing makes sure that food doesn't get stuck in her teeth or gums. Her teeth stay white and healthy. Alexis flosses every day, too. Floss is a special string that you put between your teeth. It gets food out from between your teeth. This keeps your gums healthy. Alexis knows a lot about teeth! She should know a lot. Her mom is a dentist!

Finish each sentence.

1. Alexis eats a _____ for dessert.

2. Alexis brushes her teeth _____ times a day.

3. You need to floss to keep your _____ healthy.

Earth Day

Spring is a time to really notice the earth. Leaves are growing on trees. Animals are coming out to eat and play. Every April we have a special day for honoring the earth. It is called Earth Day. But what can a kid do to help on Earth Day? Walk down your street. Do you see empty bottles on the road or sidewalk? Pick them up. The world is already better! But there's more. Don't put the bottles in a trashcan. Trash is filling up the earth. Wash and reuse the bottles instead. They can hold almost anything. You could even make a bird feeder from a bottle. You can help the air, too. Plant a small tree. The leaves on the tree take in dirty air. Then they give us clean air. Our world is a wonderful place! We just need to take care of it on Earth Day and every day.

Answer the questions below. Use the words in the word bank.

plant   April   reuse

1. When is Earth Day? _____

2. How can you clean the air? _____

3. What can you do with empty bottles? _____

A Better Breakfast

Sam has a math test today. He is feeling nervous. He's not very hungry this morning. Sam only wants something to drink. He walks into the kitchen. He opens the refrigerator. Orange juice looks just fine. Sam pours some into a glass and sits at the table. Sam's sister, Sally, enters the room. "That's not a healthy breakfast! Your stomach will be empty. How will you do on your math test then?" Sam knows that she's right. He lets her make a better breakfast for him. First, she puts bread in the toaster. Warm toast will fill him up. But Sam needs something more. She places a pan on the hot stove. She cracks two eggs into the pan. Soon the eggs are done. She puts the toast and eggs on a plate. Sam eats it all! Maybe he really was hungry. Now he will do better on his test, too.

Read each sentence. Circle *true* or *false*.

1. Sally says orange juice isn't a healthy breakfast.   true   false

2. Sam's sister toasts the bread first.   true   false

3. She bakes the eggs in the oven.   true   false

Broken Bone

Gabe made two paper airplanes. He needed someone else to play. Gabe thought of Grandpa. His house was a few blocks away. Gabe got on his bike. He had the airplanes in his backpack. Gabe rode near the side of the road. He wanted to be safe from cars, but the road was sandy there. There were rocks. Thump! Gabe lay on the road. His bike was on its side. He had fallen off the bike. His arm hurt a lot! Gabe got up and walked his bike to Grandpa's house. His arm wouldn't stop hurting. Grandpa took him to the doctor. Gabe had broken his arm. He had to wear a cast. The cast helped his arm heal. He had to wear it for two months. During that time, Gabe couldn't ride his bike, but he still flew airplanes with Grandpa. He just used the other arm!

Answer the questions below.

1. Where was Gabe going? _____

2. How did he break his arm? _____

3. How long did he wear the cast? _____

Crawling with Crickets

"Chirp-chirp-chirp! Chirp-chirp-chirp!" Are those little birds? Katie's mom says no. They are crickets. Crickets are bugs that live in the grass and trees. Katie always hears them after dinner in the summer. Crickets are very loud! Katie's mom says that they don't use their mouths to make music. They rub their two front wings together. Crickets have a lot of talent. Katie is good at some things, too. She wins hide-and-seek often. That gives Katie an idea. She calls some of her friends on the phone. Katie asks them to come over. It's warm out tonight. They can play hide-and-seek in her backyard. It will be fun! Tyler will run after them first. Katie hides behind a bush. She sees Tyler coming. She needs to move before he sees her. She crawls on the ground. She moves very quietly. Katie wants to be quieter than the crickets. It works! Tyler sees Jessica first. Katie isn't found once. Thanks, crickets!

Read each question. Circle the right answer.

1. When does Katie hear crickets?
   a. winter mornings
   b. summer evenings
   c. after lunch

2. How do crickets sing?
   a. by opening their mouths
   b. by rubbing their eyes
   c. by rubbing their wings together

3. Where does Katie play hide-and-seek?
   a. backyard   **c.** parking lot
   b. pool

4. Why does Katie win hide-and-seek?
   a. She runs fast.
   b. She is quieter than the crickets.
   c. She knows good hiding places.

All About Bats

You may know that bats live in caves. Did you know that they can live in trees or under bridges? Bats can live almost anywhere, but they don't like very cold places. You may have heard that bats drink blood. Some bats drink the blood of birds. Bats won't come after your blood, though! Most bats eat other things. They often eat fruit and nectar from flowers. Some bats fly down to the water. They catch fish for dinner. Bats are good fliers, but they are not birds. Birds have feathers and lay eggs. Bats have hair and their babies are born alive. Bats are more like people than like birds! They help people, too. Bats can spread seeds for new plants to grow. They also eat bugs. Bats hunt for food at night. To find their way in the dark, bats give off sounds. The sounds bounce off trees, rocks, and the walls of caves. The sounds bounce back to the bats. Then the bats know how far away things are. Bats are very smart animals!

Read each sentence. Circle *true* or *false*.

1. Bats can live anywhere on earth.   true   false

2. Some bats eat fish.   true   false

3. Bats are birds.   true   false

4. Sounds help bats find their way in the dark.   true   false

A New Kind of Angel

Today was a snow day! The school was closed. Olivia and Allison wanted to go sledding, but their yards were too flat. They could sled in the park instead. There are a lot of hills there. The girls put on coats, hats, boots, and gloves. They carried their sleds to the park. A lot of kids were at the park already. Some kids were sledding very fast. Olivia couldn't wait to go down the big hill. Then Allison saw other kids on the ground. Were they hurt? They were moving their arms and legs. Allison walked closer. The kids got up. They weren't hurt at all. They were making shapes in the snow. The shapes looked like angels. These were snow angels! That would be fun. Olivia came over. Allison showed her how to make the angels. The girls lay down in the snow. They moved their arms and legs out and in. They stood up carefully. Then they found more flat snow. Allison and Olivia made more snow angels. They stood up again. They made a whole family of snow angels!

Finish each sentence.

1. Olivia and Allison carried their _____ to the park.

2. They saw kids making shapes in the _____.

3. The girls moved their arms and _____ out and in.

4. They made a whole _____ of snow angels.

Raising a Rabbit

Justin had a great birthday. He got a pet rabbit! It was exactly what he wanted! He loves holding her, but he has to take care of her, too. Justin has a book about rabbits. It tells him what to do. He should have a cage for his rabbit. That is where the rabbit will sleep. She will eat there, too. Should Justin put a carrot in the cage? Rabbits need to eat more than that. They need a lot of hay. They also need water and leafy vegetables. Justin learns that rabbits make messes in their cages. The cage must be cleaned once or twice a week. He will clean the cage every Tuesday and Saturday. Rabbits need to be out of their cages sometimes. They love to run and jump. Justin must watch her because rabbits also love to hide. They also like to chew on things! She could chew the legs of a table or chair. Justin must get a chew toy for her.

Read each question. Circle the right answer.

1. What did Justin receive on his birthday?
  a. rabbit
  b. rocket
  c. hamster

2. Where does it sleep?
  a. car
  b. bed
  c. cage

3. How often should Justin clean the cage?
  a. once or twice a week
  b. once or twice a month
  c. three times a day

4. Why must Justin follow his rabbit around the house?
  a. to see if the rabbit does a trick
  b. to make sure the rabbit doesn't chew on anything
  c. to stop the rabbit from making a salad

What to Pack?

    "Destiny! We're leaving in an hour. Is your suitcase packed?" Destiny's dad calls her from downstairs. Destiny has been drawing a picture. She is imagining what Texas will look like. She hasn't packed yet. Destiny goes to her closet. She takes her suitcase out. First, she should pack clothes. She knows that Texas is hot in the summer. She folds light shirts and shorts in the suitcase. She takes sandals, too. They will be taking a train to Texas. She has never ridden on a train. Her dad says it is fun. She can watch the world go by fast. She can draw pictures of what she sees, too. Destiny puts paper and colored pencils in her suitcase. Destiny will also sleep on the train. She and her dad will have little beds! But the train will be very loud. How will she sleep? She should take some earplugs, too. Then the train will be quiet enough. Destiny drops the earplugs in her suitcase. She's all ready to go!

Answer the questions below.

1. Where is Destiny going on her trip? _____

2. What will Destiny ride? _____

3. What clothes does she pack? _____

4. Why does Destiny pack earplugs? _____

Fluffy Stuff

Are you wearing something made of cotton? Maybe it is your shirt. Look closely at it. Do you see very thin lines? These are threads. Now look even closer. You may see all the threads woven together. Today we have machines to make cotton cloth fast, but it used to take a long time. First, people had to gather cotton that grew in big fields. People picked the cotton all day. They filled as many baskets as they could. Then they turned it into thread. How did they turn fluffy balls into thin string? They would spin it. This means they would twist and twist the cotton. The cotton would get thinner and longer. Soon it would be thread. Then it was time to weave the thread together. Someone had to cross the threads. Oftentimes, a *loom* was used. A loom is a wooden square frame that helped hold many threads still and neat. They were woven tightly. Finally, it is a piece of cotton cloth! The cloth is used to sew shirts, pants, dresses, and many other kinds of clothing.

Answer the questions below. Use the words in the word bank.

> weave   field   cotton   spin

1. What is some clothing made of? _____

2. Where does cotton grow? _____

3. How do you make thread from cotton? _____

4. How do you make cloth from thread? _____

A Better Letter

Aaron received a new book from his aunt. It's about dinosaurs! He wants to thank her. Dad tells him to write a letter to her on the computer. Aaron is learning to type in school. This will give him practice. Aaron sits in front of the screen. He thinks about what to say. Then comes the hard part. He has to find the right keys. Each key is a letter. It takes him a long time to write each sentence. When he is done, the letter will look very neat. It won't have eraser marks. It's easy to erase mistakes on a computer. He just presses a special button! No one will ever know. Soon Aaron is finished typing the letter. He reads it. Nothing is spelled wrong. Then he is ready to print it. He presses another button. His letter comes out of the printer. He wants another copy. He will save it. Aaron presses the button again. Another letter comes out. That was a lot faster than writing two letters!

Finish each sentence.

1. Aaron is writing a letter on his _____.

2. He is learning to _____.

3. It's easier to _____ mistakes.

4. Aaron can print another _____ of the letter.

Baseball Wall

Jimmy and Dad will change Jimmy's bedroom. They will put up new wallpaper. Jimmy doesn't like the old wallpaper. It has teddy bears on it. His room looks like a baby's room! Jimmy wants baseballs and bats instead. First, they must take off the old wallpaper. Jimmy thinks this will be fun. He takes a corner of the wallpaper. Then he pulls as hard as he can. A big strip comes off the wall! He laughs. Jimmy pulls off the rest of the wallpaper. Next, they put up the new wallpaper. It is white, and it has blue stripes. Dad makes sure that the new wallpaper is straight. He does a good job. Now it is time for the border. The border has baseballs and bats on it. It will go across the top of the wall. Only Dad can reach that high, but he has to climb a ladder first. Then Dad puts the border on carefully. Jimmy looks up at the walls. His room looks great!

Read each sentence. Circle *true* or *false*.

1. Jimmy thinks his bedroom looks like a baby's room.   true   false

2. He and Dad are painting Jimmy's bedroom.   true   false

3. First, Jimmy pulls off the old wallpaper.   true   false

4. Dad puts up the dinosaur border.   true   false

Sister on a Skateboard

"Tie the helmet on tight!" Alexander calls out. Christina puts the helmet on her head. She loves to move fast. She rides her bike everywhere, but today she is learning to ride a skateboard. Her brother, Alexander, is teaching her. Alexander comes out of the garage. He is wearing a helmet. He is also wearing pads on his knees. He has pads for Christina, too. She must always wear them when she skateboards. She could fall and get hurt without them. Christina puts on the pads. Now she wants to skateboard! Alexander stands with one foot on his skateboard. He pushes off the ground with his other foot. The skateboard rolls forward. He keeps both feet on the board. It looks easy enough! Christina tries. She gets her skateboard to roll forward, but soon it stops. "How do I keep going?" Alexander shows her how. She must keep pushing with her foot. Christina will need that foot a lot. Alexander shows her how to drag her foot on the ground. That will slow down the skateboard. Christina doesn't ever want to slow down!

Read each question. Circle the right answer.

1. What is Christina learning to ride?
   a. a surfboard
   b. a skateboard
   c. a bicycle

2. Where does she wear pads?
   a. knees
   b. hands
   c. head

3. How does Christina stop?
   a. She jumps off the skateboard.
   b. She steps on the brake.
   c. She drags her foot on the ground.

4. Why does she like to skateboard?
   a. She likes to move fast.
   b. She likes to wear a lot of things.
   c. She likes to fall.

A Place for Pioneers

Have you heard of a pioneer? A pioneer is the first person to do something or go somewhere. Once there were a lot of pioneers in our country. These families were looking for new land. All the land on the east coast was already being used. They wanted their own land. The pioneers needed to go westward to find some. But no one had gone that way yet. They didn't know what was out west. The pioneers were brave people. They were smart, too. They brought a lot of food. They also brought animals. The animals pulled everything in wagons. The pioneers slept in the wagons, too. They traveled for many weeks. They met people who already lived on the land. These people were the Native Americans. They taught the pioneers about the land. Soon the pioneers found some land of their own. Then they built their own farms.

Answer the questions below. Use the words in the word bank.

> wagons   westward   pioneers   farms

1. Who was looking for new land? _____

2. Where did the pioneers travel? _____

3. What did the pioneers ride in? _____

4. What did they make out of the land? _____

Picking a Puppy

José wants a puppy. Puppies are so cute! They like to play. He thinks his dog Buddy wants another friend, too. They can all play catch together. His parents say okay. They take him to the animal shelter. This is a place where cats and dogs are safe. They are given food. They sleep in cages. These animals need real homes. José will adopt one of the puppies. Then he can take it home. The puppy will be his! Which puppy will be the one? José looks in the big cage. Lots of puppies are rolling around. Some are sleeping, too. They all look very soft. José likes the black puppy best. It reminds him of Buddy. Buddy is all black. Maybe Buddy will think the puppy is his baby. That's the one! José adopts the black puppy. Now he can take it home. The puppy is too young to walk that far so José carries it in his arms. It sleeps the whole time.

Answer the questions below.

1. Who wants a puppy? _____

2. Where can he adopt a puppy? _____

3. What color is his puppy? _____

4. How does he take the puppy home? _____

Weekend Away

Jennifer's parents are taking a short vacation. They are flying to a beach. Jennifer gets in the car with them, but she is not going to the airport. She is going to Faith's house. Faith is her cousin. Jennifer will be a guest at her cousin's house. That means that Jennifer will stay there. Jennifer will have fun with Faith. They will spend the whole weekend together. First, Aunt Laura makes them lunch. She cuts up vegetables for a salad. Jennifer notices one that she's never seen before. It looks like a big egg, but it's green and bumpy. Faith says that it's called an avocado. It's a fruit! Jennifer has never eaten avocado before. She wants to try it. Aunt Laura gives her a chunk. It tastes smooth and buttery. Jennifer and Faith eat the rest of the salad. Now they have all afternoon to play. What should they do? Faith says they can play school. She lets Jennifer be the teacher. Jennifer is having a great weekend vacation!

Finish each sentence.

1. Jennifer is a _____ at Faith's house.

2. She is staying for a whole _____.

3. Jennifer eats _____ for the first time.

4. They play _____ all afternoon.

Noisy Niece

"Waaah! Waaaa-aaaaah!" Brooke was crying again. Kyle was going crazy! He lived in a big house. Many other people lived there, too. His grandparents lived downstairs. His older brother and his brother's wife lived upstairs. They just had a baby. The baby was Kyle's niece. They named her Brooke. She was very small and light, but she knew how to cry! Kyle walked upstairs. He asked if he could help. Kyle held Brooke in his arms. She stopped crying. Then she fell asleep! Kyle put her down in her crib. He wanted to play his new video game next. He liked to play it loud, but he might wake up Brooke. Kyle went outside instead. He could use some fresh air. Kyle got on his bike and started to pedal. He didn't know where he would go. He kept going down the street. Soon Kyle was at the park. He rode along the paths. Then he saw a little girl in the grass. She was laughing with her dad. Kyle couldn't wait until his niece was older!

Read each question. Circle the right answer.

1. Who was crying?
   a. Brooke
   b. Kyle
   c. Kyle's brother

2. Who is a niece?
   a. your child
   b. the child of your brother or sister
   c. the child in your house

3. Why couldn't Kyle play his video game loud?
   a. because his uncle was sleeping
   b. because his niece was sleeping
   c. because he was losing his hearing

4. Where did Kyle go?
   a. to the park
   b. to the bike shop
   c. to the grocery store

Bike Safety

"Better safe than sorry!" Have you heard that before? It means that you should always do the safe thing. Then you won't get hurt. That's what bike safety is all about. Bike safety prevents you from getting hurt. You can begin to be safe even before you get on your bike. First, you should wear bright clothes. Now cars can easily see you. Make sure you have sneakers on your feet. Don't wear sandals or go barefoot! Tie your laces tight. You must also wear a helmet. Tie it to your head. Don't wear headphones. You can't hear cars if you have music in your ears. Now you are ready to ride! Are you coming out of a driveway? Stop and look for cars in both directions first. Ride near the curb of the right side of the street. This is the same direction as the cars. Do you see a stop sign or a stoplight? Do what cars do. Stop! Is the way clear? Enjoy the rest of your bike ride!

Read each sentence. Circle *true* or *false*.

1. Bike safety will prevent you from getting hurt.　　　　true　　false

2. It doesn't matter what shoes you wear.　　　　true　　false

3. Ride in the same direction as cars.　　　　true　　false

4. Always stop at stop signs.　　　　true　　false

Dear Diary

Maria wanted to measure a piece of paper, but she couldn't find her ruler. She wondered if Carlos had one. He wasn't home. He wouldn't mind if she looked in his desk. Maria opened the top drawer. She found a ruler! Under the ruler was a blue notebook. Maria had to look inside. She opened to the first page. It said, "Dear Journal." Right then Carlos walked into his room. "What are you doing, Maria? That's my journal!" Carlos was angry. Maria said she hadn't read more than two words. Then she asked Carlos about his journal. Carlos said it is a notebook for his thoughts. The journal helps him get ideas for stories. Carlos wants to be a writer someday. Maria said that she also has a notebook, but she calls her notebook a diary. She writes "Dear Diary" every night. Then she writes about what happened that day. Tonight she will write about how Carlos wants to be a writer, too.

Finish each sentence.

1. Maria was looking for a ruler in Carlos's _____.

2. _____ writes in a diary.

3. _____ writes in a journal.

4. Carlos wants to be a _____ someday.

Big Blizzard

Everyone on the bus is talking about snow. They say that a snowstorm is coming tonight. It won't be just any snowstorm. It will be a blizzard! A blizzard means that a lot of snow will fall. It will be very windy outside. We won't have school tomorrow! I can't wait to play in the snow. I think about sledding down the hill in the backyard and having a snowball fight with my sisters. We always have fun in the snow. Soon I get home. There is a note on the front door. Dad wrote that he went to the store. I go inside and eat an apple. Then Dad comes home. He has six bags of food! He says that we must prepare. We need enough food for a few days. A blizzard can close the roads. I wonder how much snow will fall. Maybe we can make tunnels in the yard! Dad says that I should have lots of fun tomorrow, but he will need my help, too. My sisters and I should shovel the driveway before we play.

Answer the questions below.

1. When is the snowstorm coming? _____

2. What is it called? _____

3. Who went shopping for food? _____

4. What should the kids do before playing in the snow? _____

Sandy Surprise

Josh and his mom are at the beach today, but they are not swimming. They are not making sand castles, either. Today they are looking for oysters. Oysters are little animals. They look like two shells put together. Oysters like to hide in the sand. Josh has to dig to find them. Then he puts the oysters in his pail. It is hard work, but Josh finds a lot of oysters. Then he brings the pail to his mom. She is cooking the oysters for dinner tonight. She needs to open them first. She uses a special knife. She opens one. There's something else inside. It is a little white ball. It's a pearl! Josh didn't know that pearls came from oysters. His mom says that pearls really come from sand. A piece of sand gets stuck inside an oyster. The oyster rolls the sand around in there. This helps the sand grow into a pearl!

Finish each sentence. Use the words in the word bank.

> pearl   oysters   sand   pail

1. Josh is gathering _____.

2. He puts them in his _____.

3. Josh's mom finds a _____ in one of them.

4. A piece of _____ starts the pearl.

Pretty Peacocks

    Is that a monster with a dozen eyes? No, it's not a monster. It's a bird! Those things that look like eyes are spots on the bird's tail feathers! This special bird is called a peacock. It is one of the largest birds that can fly. It is also one of the prettiest. Only the boy peacocks have the bright feathers. These male peacocks open their tails like fans. The feathers are blue, gold, and green. They have large spots, too. The spots look like eyes at the top of the feathers. The peacocks are looking for attention from girl peacocks. The female peacocks aren't as colorful. They are mostly brown. Peacocks sometimes gather into groups. These groups are called parties! They may look around for food. Peacocks eat bugs, fruit, and small animals. Where can you see these beautiful birds? Peacocks live in Africa, India, and Southeast Asia. Those places are far away, but sometimes you can see peacocks on farms and in zoos. Have your camera ready!

Read each question. Circle the right answer.

1. Which peacocks have bright tail feathers?
   a. all
   b. females
   c. males

2. Why do peacocks open their tails?
   a. to get attention
   b. to scare other birds
   c. to get a suntan

3. What are groups of peacocks called?
   a. flocks
   b. parties
   c. schools

4. Where wouldn't you see a peacock?
   a. farm
   b. ocean
   c. India

Chicken Soup

    "Ah-choo! Ah-choo!" Samantha has been sneezing all day. Her nose is runny, too. She is happy when the school day ends. Samantha walks home slowly. She feels terrible. Then she goes up to her room. She lies down on her bed. She picks up her book. Mom opens the door. Samantha sneezes again. Mom thinks she has a cold. She should rest this afternoon. Mom brings her a glass of orange juice. The vitamins in orange juice help fight a cold, but orange juice is the last thing she wants to drink. Samantha wants something less sweet. Mom has an idea. She goes downstairs. Samantha reads her book and falls asleep. Samantha wakes up. It is dark outside. Mom turns on the light and brings a bowl in the room. It's chicken soup. It is an old remedy for fixing a cold. Samantha eats it all. She feels better already. Her nap helped, too!

Read each sentence. Circle *true* or *false*.

1. Samantha has been coughing all day.   true   false

2. She comes home and watches television.   true   false

3. Orange juice can help fight a cold.   true   false

4. Chicken soup is a good remedy for a cold.   true   false

Another Animal

Xavier really likes tigers. He has many books and videos about them. Xavier has tiger toys, too. Tigers have always been Xavier's favorite animal, but he still hasn't seen one up close. Today he will! His parents are taking him to the zoo. Xavier talks about tigers the whole way there. Then he runs to where the tigers are. They are in a big grassy area. All the tigers are sleeping in the shade. Xavier wants to see them run. He will have to come back later. His parents take him to see the pandas. Xavier doesn't know much about them. The pandas are in a rocky place. They are eating long sticks. This food is called bamboo. Pandas have to eat a lot of it. They spend most of the day eating! Then two pandas climb the rocks. They start playing chase. They are so cute! Xavier may have a new favorite animal at the zoo.

Answer the questions below.

1. What were Xavier's favorite animals? _____

2. Where do Xavier's parents take him? _____

3. What are all the tigers doing? _____

4. What are the pandas eating? _____

Stunk Like a Skunk

Courtney saw a small animal in the front yard. It was black like Sasha. Sasha is her neighbor's cat. Sasha shouldn't be outside. Courtney should take her home. Courtney walked close to the animal. It had a white stripe. Courtney didn't remember that Sasha had a white stripe. Courtney bent to pick it up. It lifted its tail. It sprayed Courtney's hands. That wasn't Sasha. It was a skunk! Courtney should have known. Skunks are black with a white stripe. They spray to protect themselves. It didn't want Courtney to touch it. The spray really stunk! It left a bad odor on Courtney's hands. She went inside to wash it off. She used a lot of soap and water, but her hands still smelled. Her dad walked in. "What's that awful odor?" Courtney told him about the skunk. Her dad knew a trick. He filled a bowl with tomato juice. He told Courtney to wash her hands in it. It worked! Then Courtney knew never to go near a skunk again!

Finish each sentence.

1. Courtney thought she saw _____ in the yard.

2. The skunk _____ Courtney.

3. The spray left a bad _____ on her hands.

4. Courtney washed her hands in _____ juice.

Facts from Fossils

   Have you seen a dinosaur? Maybe you have seen a picture of one in a book. Maybe you have seen a movie or TV show that uses a machine that looks like a dinosaur. But dinosaurs lived before humans. How do we know what they looked like? We have good imaginations! We also study fossils. These are what dinosaurs left behind. Bones, teeth, and even skin can turn into fossils. They are buried under the ground. We find these small pieces of a dinosaur's body. Then we put the pieces together. We can learn a lot from fossils. We know that Tyrannosaurus rex was twelve feet tall. That is three times taller than you! It must have needed a lot of food. Tyrannosaurus rex had a lot of sharp teeth. It must have eaten meat. We think that it ate other dinosaurs. Tyrannosaurus rex had to catch these smaller dinosaurs so it must have lived near them. Many smaller dinosaurs ate leaves and plants. They lived in warm forests. We can guess that Tyrannosaurus rex lived in forests, too. Fossils tell us so much!

Finish each sentence. Use the words in the word bank.

dinosaurs   fossils   bodies   forests

1. We learn from the _____ that dinosaurs left behind.

2. Fossils are what remains of their _____.

3. Tyrannosaurus rex ate other _____.

4. Tyrannosaurus rex lived in warm _____.

April Fool

Jackson likes to play little tricks. He never hurts anyone, but he always gets in trouble. That's why he loves April Fools' Day. It happens on the first day of every April. It's a day for playing jokes. The person who is tricked is called an April Fool. This is Jackson's favorite holiday! This year he is playing a trick on his sister Hannah. He sneaks into her room at night. Hannah is sleeping. He turns her clock back one hour. She doesn't hear him. She wakes up when her alarm clock beeps. Hannah takes a shower, gets dressed, and eats breakfast. Then she walks outside and waits for the bus. She waits and waits. Hannah looks at her watch. It says 7:30. The bus comes at 8:30. She hears Jackson laughing behind her. "I changed your alarm clock! April Fool!" Hannah laughs, too. She will play a good trick on him later!

Read each question. Circle the right answer.

1. When is Jackson's favorite holiday?
   a. December
   b. April
   c. August

2. Who does he play a trick on?
   a. his sister
   b. his cat
   c. his mom

3. What causes Hannah to be early for the bus?
   a. She doesn't hear her alarm clock.
   b. She takes a long shower.
   c. Jackson changes the time on her clock.

4. What will Hannah do later on?
   a. play a trick on Jackson
   b. get a new alarm clock
   c. forget about April Fools' Day

Brianna's Brother

Brianna opens the newspaper. There is a story about a boy in town. The headline says that he helps older people. Her brother Mike does that, too. She starts reading the story. It's about Mike! The story talks about how Mike visits his grandmother every day. He makes her dinner. He plays cards with her. They read books together. Mike's visits make his grandmother happy. She told Mike about other older people on her street. They don't have anyone visiting them. Mike wanted to help them, too. He started visiting a different person every night. He helps clean their homes. He listens to their stories. The reporter asked the older people about Mike. They all said that he is a big help. He is also fun to have around. What a great story! Brianna closes the newspaper. Mike walks in the room. He has a large piece of paper in his hands. Mike received an award. It is from the mayor. She read the newspaper story, too. She wanted to thank him for his kindness.

Read each sentence. Circle *true* or *false*.

1. Brianna sees the news story on TV.   true   false

2. Mike has been helping older people.   true   false

3. The older people don't like him.   true   false

4. Mike receives an award because of his kindness.   true   false

A Melted Mess

Paige worked hard on her book report this week. She read a book about grasshoppers. Then she wrote about what she learned. Paige knows her teacher will like the report. She reads her report once more while she eats breakfast. Paige makes sure not to get crumbs on the report. Then she goes upstairs to get dressed. She leaves the report on the table. She leaves the butter there, too. The butter starts to melt in the sun. It turns into a liquid. It spreads across the table. It smears her report! Then Paige sees the mess. She doesn't have time to write another report! She wipes off as much butter as she can. Then she brings it to school. She hands the messy report to her teacher. Paige hopes that she will receive a great grade, anyway. But she doesn't. Paige feels sad. She worked so hard. She should have been more careful that morning. Paige won't leave butter out ever again!

Write an effect to each cause on the chart.

Cause	Effect
1. Paige leaves the butter on the table.	
2. She leaves her report near the butter.	
3. Paige hands in the messy report.	
4. She feels sad about the grade.	

The Tale of Braille

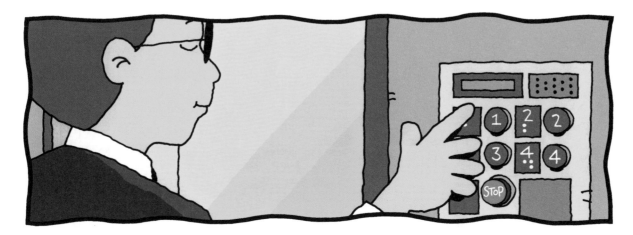

What if you lost your eyesight? You would be blind. How could you read? Life wouldn't be as much fun without books! Louis Braille invented a way for blind people to read. He went blind when he was very young. His parents sent him to a special school. Other blind kids learned there, too. It was hard for them to read. The books had raised letters, but it wasn't easy to feel them. Louis had a great idea. The books should use raised dots instead of letters. Each group of dots was one letter. The system of dots was easy to learn and use. It was called the *Braille system*. Louis was an inventor when he was only fifteen years old! His system is still used all over the world. Blind people can read anything now. Look closely when you are in an elevator. You may even see his dots on the buttons!

Answer the questions below.

1. What is hard for blind people to do? _____

2. What happened to Louis Braille when he was young? _____

_____

3. What did he invent? _____

4. Where might you see the raised dots? _____

Scared of Slides

Splash! Splash! Water sounds are everywhere. Evan is at a park, but not just any park. He is at a water park! Evan watches families play in the water. Some kids are floating on tubes. Others are swimming in the wave pool. Evan wants to spend all day in the pool, but his best friend, Nate, wants to ride the slides. Nate points to the tall red one. Evan sees all the turns in the slide. Then he watches kids come out the bottom. They are going so fast! And there are so many stairs to climb first! Evan is scared, but Nate really wants to try the slide together. Evan says okay. Nate walks him up the stairs. Evan holds onto Nate's arm. Then Nate goes down the slide. Evan hears him scream with delight. Now it's Evan's turn. Evan lets the water carry him down. "Wheeeee!" His body moves so fast. He is having fun! He forgets to hold his nose shut at the end. Water goes up his nose, but Evan wants to try the next slide!

Finish each sentence.

1. Evan is at the _____ park.

2. He is _____ to ride the tall slide.

3. _____ walks Evan up the stairs.

4. Water goes up his _____ because he doesn't hold it shut.

Brown Bananas

Kaitlyn turned ten years old yesterday. Now she is old enough to pack her own lunch. Today she makes it for the first time. First, she puts together her favorite sandwich. Kaitlyn places turkey, lettuce, and mustard between bread. Then she fills a bag with baby carrots. She wants fruit, too. In the bowl is her favorite fruit! She takes a banana and peels it. Kaitlyn cuts it into slices and puts them in a bag. She takes her lunch to school. Kaitlyn can't wait to eat it. The sandwich is so good. The carrots are crunchy. But the bananas are brown! They were yellow before. What happened? Her teacher knows. Bananas are yellow until they are peeled. Then they turn brown in the air. Kaitlyn's banana slices have never turned brown before! That's because her mom knows a trick. She puts lemon juice on the slices. The juice keeps them yellow. Kaitlyn has a lot to learn about making lunch.

Answer the questions below. Use the words in the word bank.

> lemon   brown   lunch   banana

1. What does Kaitlyn make for the first time? _____

2. What is Kaitlyn's favorite fruit? _____

3. What color do the banana slices turn? _____

4. What kind of juice keeps bananas yellow? _____

The Last Game

Jacob is a great basketball player. He plays on the school team. His team wins almost every game. The last game is on Monday. They are playing against the hardest team. Jacob wants to win! He practices all weekend. His dad helps him. Jacob dribbles, passes, and shoots the basketball in his driveway. He runs to the park and back. Then Jacob notices that his lucky sneakers are falling apart. He should get some new sneakers. He buys a white and red pair. Jacob wears them to the big game. He plays well. He doesn't miss one basket. Then the score is tied. The clock is running out of time. Jacob needs to go fast. He runs down the court. He jumps as high as he can. He pushes the basketball into the net. His team wins! Jacob says he made the last basket because of his new shoes. His dad says he is wrong. Jacob did it because he practiced so hard.

Read each sentence. Circle *true* or *false*.

1. Jacob wants to win the last basketball game.   true   false

2. He wears his lucky sneakers.   true   false

3. Jacob makes the last basket.   true   false

4. His team wins only because of Jacob's new sneakers.   true   false

Cheetah Chase

Pedal your bicycle as hard as you can. How fast can you go? It feels very fast. Did you know that a cat can travel even faster? This cat is called a cheetah. It is one of the big cats. Other big cats are lions and tigers. They all live in the wild. It is easy to recognize a cheetah. It has yellow fur with black spots. Cheetahs live on *savannas*. These are open plains with lots of grass. There are savannas in Africa. A lot of other animals live there, too. Cheetahs eat rabbits and antelope. Antelope are like deer. Cheetahs can chase and catch them for food. Cheetahs are great runners. They are the fastest animals on land over short distances. They can still be hunted, though. Sometimes people shoot and kill them for fun. The cheetah's food is running out, too. Cheetahs are in danger of dying out!

Read each question. Circle the right answer.

1. How can you recognize a cheetah?
  a. its black and white stripes
  b. its black spots
  c. its yellow spots

2. Where do cheetahs live?
  a. savannas
  b. oceans
  c. farms

3. What do cheetahs eat?
  a. cheese puffs
  b. peanut butter and jelly
  c. rabbits and antelope

4. Which is **not** a reason for cheetahs dying out?
  a. People hunt them for fun.
  b. They are freezing in the snow.
  c. They are running out of food.

Rainy Day

Luke looks out the window. It's raining outside! That means he can't play in the grass today. He will have to stay inside. His younger sister wants to play a game. Sophia says the game is like being at school, but Luke doesn't want to be at school! Sophia says the game will be fun. Luke says he will play if he can be the teacher. Sophia agrees. Luke says that math class is first. He writes a math test on a piece of paper. Sophia must add and subtract large numbers. That's not fair! She doesn't know how to do the test. She is only in kindergarten. Luke says that they should play another game. He finds a deck of cards. He wants to play Go Fish. Luke teaches Sophia how to play. She must make pairs of cards. Luke wins three times. Sophia wins three times, too. This game is much more fun!

Finish each sentence.

1. They are staying _____ because it is raining outside.

2. _____ wants to play school.

3. Luke writes a _____ test.

4. _____ wants to play Go Fish.

5. They each win _____ times.

Gift for Gabby

Morgan's best friend is Gabby. Last week Morgan and Gabby were shopping with Gabby's mom. Gabby saw a silver necklace that she liked. The necklace gave Morgan an idea. She had some money saved. She would use it to buy Gabby the necklace as a birthday gift. But as Morgan was walking to the shop, she slipped and fell on the sidewalk. Some of her quarters rolled away. They fell down a grate! Now she would not have enough money to buy the necklace. Morgan looked at everything else in the store. There were silver earrings, too. Morgan bought the earrings instead. Then she went home and wrapped the gift. She took it to Gabby's birthday party. Gabby opened Morgan's gift. Gabby loved the silver earrings. Her mom gave her the necklace earlier that day. Now Gabby had a matching set! Morgan never thought that she would feel lucky to lose money.

Answer the questions below.

1. What had Morgan been saving? _____

2. What caused her to lose the quarters? _____

3. What did Morgan buy Gabby instead? _____

4. Who bought Gabby the necklace? _____

5. How does Morgan feel? _____

Value of Video Games

Luis loves to be outside. He plays baseball in the spring and soccer in the fall. Luis stays in shape. But his brother Billy isn't like Luis. Billy doesn't like sports too much. He would rather sit inside and play with his video games. Billy spends all his free time playing these games. He gets a lot of practice with the controller. Now he can move his hands really fast. That skill helps him one day when Luis wants to play ping-pong. Luis thinks he will win because he is better at sports. But Billy can move the paddle so fast! Billy wins four games in a row. Luis can't believe it. Maybe video games have value too. Luis goes inside and tries one. While Luis uses the game, Billy has to do something else. He decides to go to the store to buy another video game! Billy gets on his bicycle. He has to stop halfway to the store. He gets tired so fast! Maybe Billy needs to get more exercise.

Answer the questions below.

1. What sport does Luis play in the spring? _____

2. What does Billy like to do? _____

3. What game do Luis and Billy play together? _____

4. Why does Billy stop riding his bicycle halfway to the store? _____

_____

Safe in the Sun

Has anyone told you to stay out of the sun or you'll get burned? It's true. It doesn't matter how dark your skin is. You can even get burned on a cloudy day. You can get burned sitting in the shade. Did you know that rays of the sun can burn in the winter, too? But the rays are strongest in the summer. Clothing will protect you from the sun's rays. You should wear long-sleeved shirts and pants. Put a hat on your head. This will protect your face and the top of your head. What if it's much too hot to wear these clothes? Then you should use sunscreen. Sunscreen is a cream that you apply on your skin. It blocks the sun's rays. Try to buy a bottle of waterproof sunscreen. It won't wash off when you swim or sweat. Apply sunscreen often if you spend a long time outdoors. Go inside if your skin starts to look pink or red. Be careful in the sun and you won't get burned!

Answer the questions below. Use the words in the word bank.

red   waterproof   summer   rays   hat

1. What can burn your skin? _____

2. When is the sun the strongest? _____

3. What kind of sunscreen protects you when you swim? _____

4. What should you wear on your head? _____

5. Go inside if your skin looks this color. _____

Hot Cake

Brandon almost forgot about Grandma's birthday! Her birthday is today. He told Mom that he would make the cake. Now he has only a few hours. First, he rides his bicycle to the store. He buys a box of vanilla cake mix and a tub of chocolate frosting. This cake will be so good! Brandon rides home as fast as he can. He runs into the kitchen. He stirs the mix and the eggs. Next, he pours it all into a pan. Then he puts the pan in the hot oven. Phew! The cake is done after a half hour. Brandon wants to frost it now. He takes a dull knife. Brandon starts spreading the frosting on the cake. But the frosting is melting! The chocolate frosting is all over the table and soaking into the cake. Brandon didn't read the directions. He needed to wait for the cake to cool first. Now the cake is ruined. What will he do? Brandon pedals his bicycle to the store very fast. He buys a pretty cake. But he wants Grandma to know it is from him. He finds cake gel at home. Then he writes "Happy Birthday" on the cake. Brandon hopes she will like it!

Read each sentence. Circle *true* or *false*.

1. Brandon's birthday is today.   true   false

2. First, Brandon bakes the cake.   true   false

3. The frosting melts because the cake is too cold.   true   false

4. Brandon gives Grandma the cake, anyway.   true   false

5. Brandon writes with gel on the cake.   true   false

Rebecca in France

Rebecca went all the way to France! France is a country that is far away. She had to go across an ocean. Rebecca rode an airplane. The plane landed and she was in a strange place. People didn't speak English. They spoke French. Rebecca made sure to pack her French wordbook! First, she walked to the Eiffel Tower. It is made of metal bars. It looks like a very tall and thin pyramid. Rebecca rode to the top of the Eiffel Tower. She saw the pretty river and city below. Then she wanted to walk around the city. Rebecca walked down some narrow streets. A lot of people rode bicycles or small motorcycles. But Rebecca liked to go slow. She passed by the stone homes and buildings. She looked inside the small shops. She crossed many short bridges over the river. Rebecca even saw some clowns! They were doing tricks right in the street. Many people gathered to watch them. Rebecca felt very tired at the end of the day. But there was more walking to do tomorrow!

Read each question. Circle the right answer.

1. Where did Rebecca go on vacation?
   a. France
   b. a farm
   c. England

2. How did she get there?
   a. on a train
   b. on a boat
   c. on an airplane

3. What did she see first?
   a. Sears Tower
   b. Eiffel Tower
   c. Tower of France

4. What caused Rebecca to feel very tired?
   a. a lot of swimming
   b. a lot of walking
   c. a lot of sitting

5. What is another good title for this story?
   a. "France on Foot"
   b. "Clown Day"
   c. "The Eiffel Tower"

Karate Class

Almost all of Isaiah's friends take karate. They take a class once a week. They show Isaiah what they learn. Isaiah wants to kick and jump too! But Dad says that Isaiah could get hurt. Isaiah could also hurt someone else. Isaiah still wants to learn. He goes to the library. He borrows a book about karate. The book tells about some of the moves. It also shows pictures of them. But the book says that you need a class to really learn karate. Isaiah shows the book to Dad. Dad reads about the moves and the classes. He also reads about the meaning of karate. He learns that karate teaches respect for other people. Now Dad thinks that Isaiah may learn karate. He buys Isaiah a white robe and a white belt. This is what Isaiah will wear to karate class. Isaiah can't wait!

Finish each sentence.

1. Isaiah wants to learn _____.

2. He shows a karate _____ to Dad.

3. Karate teaches _____ for other people.

4. Dad buys him a white _____ and robe.

5. Isaiah can't _____!

A Lot of Lefties

"Lefty" is a nickname for a left-handed person. Are you a lefty? Do you know any? Think about your family or kids in your class. One out of every ten people is a lefty. The rest are righties. That's still a lot of lefties. Lefties are born that way. But many years ago teachers tried to change lefties. Teachers forced kids to use their right hands instead. Now lefties can use their left hands all they want. Lefties even have special desks and scissors. These make life easier for lefties. Lots of people think that lefties are very good at art and music. There is even a special holiday for lefties! August 13 is Left-Handers Day. If you want to celebrate with some lefties, go to the zoo. Some people think all polar bears are lefties!

Read each sentence. Circle *true* or *false*.

1. This passage is about right-handed people. true false

2. There are more righties than lefties. true false

3. Lefties are born that way. true false

4. Lefties need special plates for eating. true false

5. There is a holiday for lefties in the summer. true false

Cathy's Catch

"But it's still dark out, Papa!" says Cathy when her grandfather wakes her up. It is before sunrise. He says they must start early. Cathy puts on her clothes and eats some oatmeal. Then they walk to the lake. Cathy and Papa get in the fishing boat. Papa rows the boat to the middle of the lake. Cathy puts worms on the hooks at the ends of the fishing lines. She can do it even in the dark. Now the fishing rods are ready. Cathy and Papa make a good team! Each of them takes a fishing rod. They throw their lines into the water. They wait for fish. The sun starts to come up. Cathy feels a tug on her line. It must be a fish! Cathy tries to pull the line out of the water, but she can't. The fish is too strong! It gives a big pull. Cathy's feet slip. She goes overboard! Now she is swimming in the lake. Cathy and Papa laugh! That fish got away. Papa lifts her back into the boat. What is on her arm? It's a bracelet. Someone must have lost it in the lake. Cathy caught something after all!

Answer the questions below.

1. When does Cathy wake up? _____

2. Where is Cathy fishing? _____

3. What does she do first on the boat? _____

4. Why does Cathy fall in the water? _____

5. What did Cathy catch? _____

Fun Fourth of July

"Happy Fourth of July!" Garrett loves to hear those words. The Fourth of July is his favorite holiday. It celebrates when our country won freedom from England. It happens on the fourth day of July! Every year, Garrett's family goes to the big parade downtown. Colorful bands march down the middle of the street. Their music is fast and joyful. Garrett waves a small flag in the air. Then Garrett and his family go home. They have a cookout. Garrett's dad makes vegetable salad. Garrett makes a plate of hot dogs and hamburgers to be grilled. Garrett's mom makes a big cake. Garrett watches her decorate it. She uses white frosting. She arranges blueberries and strawberries on top. The cake looks like our country's flag! Their friends and neighbors love the food. Everyone has fun all afternoon. Then it gets dark. Everyone walks to the park. Now comes Garrett's favorite part of the day. He loves the fireworks! The colors explode in the sky. Boom! Boom!

Answer the questions below. Use the words in the word bank.

fireworks   July   country   parade   flag

1. When is Garrett's favorite holiday? _____

2. What is his favorite part of the day? _____

3. What does Garrett watch that morning? _____

4. What won freedom on that day? _____

5. What does the cake look like? _____

Haunted House

Emily and Christopher have a haunted house on their street! The house is old and gray. It doesn't look like anyone has lived there for a long time. There must be a ghost inside. But none of their friends has seen this ghost. Emily and Christopher want to be the first ones! But they are both scared. They flip a coin. Christopher calls tails. Emily calls heads. The coin lands on heads. She wins. Emily tells Christopher to knock on the door of the house. Christopher is shaking as he walks to the front door. He knocks once. He knocks again. The door is opening! An old man is standing there. That's not a ghost! The man says hello. Christopher looks surprised. The man laughs. "I bet you thought it was haunted! I'm just too old to fix the outside of the house." Christopher and Emily are glad to know the truth.

Read each question. Circle the right answer.

1. Who is scared of the gray house?
  a. Christopher
  b. Emily
  c. both of them

2. Why should anyone be scared of it?
  a. Because it is old and could be haunted.
  b. Because it could be a monster instead of a house.
  c. Because all gray houses are scary.

3. How do they decide who knocks on the door?
  a. They draw straws.
  b. They flip a coin.
  c. Christopher says he will do it.

4. Who answers the door?
  a. an old man
  b. a ghost
  c. Emily

5. What is another good title for this story?
  a. "I Like Ghosts"
  b. "Ghost in the Gray House"
  c. "Christopher's Sister"

Learning About the Library

      Your report is due on Monday! You are writing about turtles. But you don't know much about them. You will need to do research. You want to look up facts about turtles in books. But today is Saturday. Your school is closed. You can't get inside the school library. What will you do? You can go to the public library. That is a library that everyone can use. It is open on the weekends. The library is filled with books about every subject. You find the section with books about turtles. There are so many! You can't read them all at the library. You can take them home. The library lets you borrow the books. But you will have to return them in a few days. Do you have a library card? It helps the library know which books you borrow. You can get a card at the front desk. You will see magazines and newspapers at the library, too. Look for nature magazines. They may have an article about turtles. You can make a copy of the article. That one you may keep!

Finish each sentence. Use the words in the word bank.

> public   magazines   research   card   borrow

1. A library is a good place to do _____.

2. Everyone can go to a _____ library.

3. Libraries have books, newspapers, and _____.

4. You can _____ books instead of buying them.

5. Don't forget to bring your library _____!

Mackenzie the Clown

Mackenzie was a silly girl. She liked to tell jokes. She liked to play jokes, too. Maybe she could grow up to be a clown! Mackenzie just had to learn how to be one.

So she went to see the circus that summer. She needed to study the clowns. Mackenzie watched them juggle. Some clowns walked on a tightrope. They pretended that they were about to fall. But the clowns always stayed on the rope. And then she saw a clown riding a bicycle. The bicycle had only one wheel. Her mom said it was called a unicycle. Mackenzie wanted to ride one of those! Her mom agreed to buy her a unicycle that week. Mackenzie tried to ride it in the driveway. But she fell off every time! Mackenzie couldn't keep her balance. She wouldn't be that kind of clown. Next, Mackenzie tried to juggle. She took three oranges. She tried to keep them all in the air. But they always dropped to the ground. Then her dog ran by and stole an orange! Mackenzie wouldn't be that kind of clown, either. But her mom told her to keep practicing. And she did. Mackenzie did become a clown when she grew up!

Read each sentence. Circle *true* or *false*.

1. Mackenzie wanted to be a clown
   when she grew up.   true   false

2. She saw a unicycle on TV.   true   false

3. Mackenzie couldn't balance well.   true   false

4. She tried the tightrope.   true   false

5. This story is about how Mackenzie practiced
   to make her dreams come true.   true   false

Hats on Heads

   Summer is almost here! Jeremy and Jada need to wear hats that will protect them in the hot sun. So Dad takes them to the hat shop. The shop has at least one hundred hats! There must be every kind of hat. Jeremy sees some top hats. They are tall and black. Then he sees a cowboy hat. He tries it on. It's too big. Jada thinks he looks silly. Jeremy finds the smaller hats. He sees one with blue and red stripes. It fits! Dad says that the hat is made of wool. It is made for the winter. The hat would be too hot in the summer. But Jeremy still wants the hat. Dad buys it for him. Jada picks a hat, too. She gets a sun hat. It has a big brim. The hat has pink and yellow flowers. Jeremy and Jada wear their hats on the way home. Jeremy's head gets sweaty. Maybe the hat really is too warm for summer!

Answer the questions below.

1. Where does Dad take Jeremy and Jada? _____

2. What time of year will they use the hats? _____

3. What kind of hat does Jeremy try on first? _____

4. What kind of hat does Jada get? _____

5. What happens to Jeremy's head later? _____

Ants for Abby

Abby loves to watch ants. One day Abby came home with a spelling test. She got a perfect score! So Abby's parents had a surprise. They bought an ant farm for her! She could watch ants every day. Abby couldn't wait to set up the farm. She opened the package of ants too fast. The ants spilled everywhere! They were walking all over the kitchen floor. Abby had to catch them. She cut up a tiny piece of apple and put it in a cup. She placed the cup sideways on the floor. All of the ants walked toward the cup. They walked inside. They wanted to eat the apple. Abby picked up the cup and carefully let the ants into the ant farm. She put the apple in, too. They ate and ate! Then they dug tunnels in the sand. Abby watched them through the glass all afternoon.

Read each question. Circle the right answer.

1. Why did Abby's parents buy an ant farm?
   a. Because Abby did well on her test.
   b. Because Abby likes ants.
   c. Because Abby's parents like ants.

2. Where did all the ants go at first?
   a. in the ant farm
   b. in Abby's food
   c. on the floor

3. How did Abby gather the ants?
   a. She called their names.
   b. She put a piece of apple in a cup.
   c. She picked them up with her fingers.

4. What did Abby watch the ants do?
   a. make dinner
   b. take a bath
   c. dig tunnels

5. What is another good title for this story?
   a. "Fun with Apples"
   b. "Abby's Ant Farm"
   c. "Spelling Tests"

Pirate Life

Pirates lived on ships. They broke the law and robbed other ships. Pirates stole gold, silver, knives, and even food. Sometimes they had to wait for months to find a ship to rob. While they waited, the pirates had work to do! The pirate captain was busy driving the ship. The quartermaster gave out other jobs. Some pirates washed the decks of the ship. Others repaired broken sails and other parts of the ship. But some pirates got bored. They would start fights with other pirates. To make things worse, their food was terrible. Ships didn't have refrigerators. They couldn't have fresh food. They ate dried meat and stale bread. Yuck! Pirates couldn't drink from the ocean. The seawater has too much salt. But the ships couldn't carry much fresh water. So the pirates drank beer and wine instead. Pirates didn't bathe in the ocean, either. They got very dirty and smelly. Pirates kept their clothes on until they fell off! Would you have wanted to be a pirate?

Read each sentence. Circle *true* or *false*.

1. Pirates stole gold and silver every day.   true   false

2. The quartermaster gave the pirates jobs to do.   true   false

3. Pirates drank water from the sea.   true   false

4. They didn't bathe in the sea.   true   false

5. A pirate's life wasn't always fun.   true   false

Circus Animals

The whole town is very happy. The circus has come to their town for one day! Almost everyone is going to see the circus. People stand in line to buy tickets. Once they go inside, they buy peanuts. They are fun to crack open. They are also tasty. But some kids just want to feed them to the elephants later. Everyone finds their seats. The adults make sure that the kids can see everything. The show begins! A woman rides on an elephant. She is the animal tamer. She can tell any animal what to do. Then the cages appear. Each cage has a tiger inside. The tigers look dangerous. The tamer lets them out. But the tigers stay calm and still. Then she raises her arms. All the tigers stand on two legs! Later she tells a seal to balance a ball on its nose. She waves her hand. Two monkeys ride bikes around the ring. Finally, she gives a signal. All the elephants do a silly dance. Everyone claps. They throw yummy peanuts to reward the hungry elephants.

Finish each sentence.

1. The circus is in town for one _____.

2. Kids want to feed the _____.

3. There is a _____ in each cage.

4. The tamer tells the tigers to _____.

5. Two monkeys ride _____.

Lucky Puck

Kevin attends all of his brother's hockey games. Kevin watches from the stands. Hockey looks like a hard sport. The players have to hit a small puck with their sticks. And they have to do it on ice! Kevin wants to play hockey one day, too. He will watch his brother for now. His brother is a great player. His team likes to pass the puck to him. He stops it with his stick. Kevin cheers. Suddenly, his brother swings the stick fast. Is the black puck gone? No one sees it on the ice. That's because the puck is flying through the air! That must be a lucky puck. The puck lands right near the goal. The other team is still looking for the puck. The puck slides into the goal. The clock runs out of time. Kevin's brother just made the final point! Kevin feels very proud.

Answer the questions below. Use the words in the word bank.

puck   sport   point   ice   swing

1. Kevin watches the teams play on the _____.

2. Hockey is a hard _____.

3. Kevin's brother can _____ his stick fast.

4. The black _____ flies through the air.

5. Kevin's brother makes the final _____.

Class in the Grass

Mia stands in the grass. She raises her hands in the air. She lifts her right leg out and bends to the left. Her arms land on the grass. Her legs are in the air. She lets her feet land on the grass. She is now standing again. Mia loves to do cartwheels! Mia wants to learn to do back flips, too. So Mia's mom takes her to a tumbling class. The first class is about cartwheels. Mia can already do those! The teacher brings out a balance beam. It is narrow and high off the ground. The class walks across the beam. A few kids fall. They land on a soft mat. The teacher says that they will do cartwheels across the beam soon. Mia is scared. She doesn't want to fall off the beam. She could land on her head! She wants to practice at home first. She finds a long piece of wood. It is smooth. Then she places it on the soft grass. This is a safe place to practice.

Read each question. Circle the right answer.

1. What can Mia do in the grass?
   a. dance
   b. cartwheel
   c. play catch

2. Where does Mia's mom take her?
   a. tumbling class
   b. dance class
   c. math class

3. Why is she afraid to cartwheel on the balance beam?
   a. It feels too rough.
   b. She is afraid to fall.
   c. She is afraid to balance.

4. How does Mia practice?
   a. She takes the balance beam home.
   b. She learns to walk on the beam first.
   c. She places a piece of wood on the grass.

5. What will happen if Mia falls off the wood?
   a. She will hit her head on the driveway.
   b. She will land on the soft grass.
   c. She will never want to use a balance beam.

All About Acorns

Have you seen an acorn before? An acorn is a nut with a cap on top. It doesn't look like a fruit. But an acorn is the fruit part of an oak tree. Acorns fall from oak trees in the summer and fall. You might see acorns on the ground if the animals don't get them first! Many animals eat acorns. You may have seen squirrels taking acorns. A bird called a woodpecker likes them, too. Deer and bears also eat acorns. Inside every acorn is a seed. This seed can grow into a new oak tree. In fact, you can use an acorn to grow your own oak tree. Gather some green acorns during the fall. Put them in a pail of water. Take the acorns that sink to the bottom. Put them in a plastic bag with some sawdust. Place the bag in the refrigerator. Wait until the acorns crack open. The roots will show. Now you can plant them in soil. Make sure the root is facing down. Water them every few days. One day you will have your own little oak tree!

Answer the questions below.

1. What part of the oak tree is an acorn? _____

2. What kind of bird likes to eat acorns? _____

3. How many seeds does each acorn have? _____

4. If you want to grow an oak tree, what should you gather in the fall? _____
_____

5. What will show when your acorn cracks open? _____

Emily's Ears

Miguel moved to a new house last week. He met his neighbors. One neighbor is his age. Her name is Emily. But they won't be in the same class. She goes to a different school. It is a school for deaf kids. These kids can't hear anything. But they can still do everything else. He sees how Emily talks with her family. She moves her hands into different positions. Each position means a different word or idea. This is called sign language. Emily moves her hands so fast. Miguel doesn't know if he can do it, too. But he wants to be friends with her. Emily's mom says they can still be friends. Miguel doesn't need to know sign language. He can just speak a little more slowly. Emily can read lips. She can watch Miguel's mouth move and know what he is saying! Emily can respond by shaking her head or pointing to things. Later Miguel tries to be deaf like Emily. He turns the TV on. Then he turns the sound off. He sees the people talking. He tries to read their lips. Miguel can't figure it out! Emily has a lot of talent.

Read each sentence. Circle *true* or *false*.

1. Miguel is deaf.   true   false

2. Emily uses sign language to talk.   true   false

3. Miguel and Emily are in the same class.   true   false

4. Miguel and Emily can be friends.   true   false

5. Miguel can understand the TV if he turns the sound off.   true   false

Rules of the Road

My brother Devin is in high school. He just turned sixteen years old. Now he can learn to drive a car. Mom took Devin for his first lesson yesterday. They let me come, too. We went to the high school parking lot. The lot was empty because it was Saturday. Devin wouldn't hit any cars. Mom showed him the basic idea of driving. The car went faster if Devin pressed the gas pedal. The car slowed down if Devin pressed the brake. Devin drove around the lot for a while. He did well! Next, Devin was ready for the road. Mom told Devin to leave the parking lot and turn left on Main Street. Devin turned the wheel. The car turned, too. Devin looked nervous. But Mom told him just to go slowly. Soon we saw a red light. Devin stopped the car. We waited for the light to turn green. But it started to rain. Devin could hardly see. Mom showed Devin the wipers. He turned them on. Then he could see and drive, too. Devin was glad to have Mom as a teacher.

Write a cause or an effect to each item on the chart.

Cause	Effect
1. Devin presses the brake.	
2.	The car goes faster.
3. Devin sees a red light.	
4. Devin turns the wheel.	
5.	Devin can see through the rain.

Soda Spray

What a hot day! Vicky was sweaty and very thirsty. She went into the kitchen for a drink. She looked in the refrigerator. Some soda sounded good. She picked up the big bottle. Plonk! It slipped from her sweaty hand. It fell onto the hard floor. Vicky remembered what happened last time she dropped a bottle of soda. She had picked up the bottle and opened it. Soda had sprayed everywhere. What a mess! Vicky wouldn't do that again. She put the bottle back in the refrigerator. She drank some juice instead. Then she went back outside. Soon her sister Kimmy wanted something cold, too. She could make an ice cream soda! First she took vanilla ice cream from the freezer. She scooped some into a tall glass. Next, she needed the soda. She took the bottle out of the refrigerator. Kimmy put her hand on the cap. That's when Vicky walked in. "Stop! Don't open it!"

Read each question. Circle the right answer.

1. What did Vicky drop on the floor?
   a. bottle of soda
   b. bottle of juice
   c. glass of soda

2. Why didn't she open it?
   a. It was dirty.
   b. It could explode.
   c. She wanted juice instead.

3. Who came in the kitchen next?
   a. Kimmy
   b. Kaylee
   c. Courtney

4. What did she start to make?
   a. ice cream sandwich
   b. cheese sandwich
   c. ice cream soda

5. What would happen if Kimmy opened the soda?
   a. There would be nothing in the bottle.
   b. The soda would spray everywhere.
   c. Nothing would happen.

Thomas Edison

Thomas Edison was born more than two hundred years ago. He attended school when he was a kid. He did poorly in class. That was because he had bad hearing. He stopped going to school and started working a job. He sold newspapers. Thomas began playing with the machines that printed the newspapers. He was always imagining new machines. Thomas became an inventor. He was one of the most famous inventors ever! He spent his whole life making new things. He made about one thousand inventions. He invented a new kind of battery. A battery gives things the power to work. Thomas invented a machine to play movies. He also invented the phonograph. It plays music records. Records were an early kind of CD. Would there be CDs today if Thomas hadn't invented the phonograph? Maybe not! But Thomas's most famous invention is the light bulb. Can you imagine life before there were light bulbs? People had to use candles and gas lamps instead. They were not very bright, and these could blow out easily. Light bulbs stay lit for a long time. Thank you, Thomas!

Answer the questions below. Use the words in the word bank.

| thousand | music | inventor | hearing | light bulb |

1. Why did Thomas Edison do poorly in school? _____

2. What is he known as today? _____

3. About how many inventions did Thomas make? _____

4. What can we now record and listen to? _____

5. What is Thomas Edison's most famous invention? _____

Sleepover Party

Isaac's mom says he can stay at Julian's house tonight. This is their first sleepover party! Isaac eats his dinner as fast as he can. Then he packs his sleep clothes and a toothbrush. His dad drives him to Julian's house. Isaac and Julian watch a movie. It is about ghosts on a farm. They share a big bowl of popcorn, too. When the movie ends, they are stuffed. They are also scared! Isaac wants to think about something else. He says they should play a board game. Julian picks one from the closet. They play for a while. Then Julian wants to play a video game! Julian and Isaac each take a controller. They sit in front of the TV. Each of them is a monster. They fight each other on the screen. Isaac wins! He cheers. Julian tells him to be quiet. His parents will wake up if they are too loud. Then Julian and Isaac will have to go to sleep. They don't want to ruin the sleepover party!

Finish each sentence.

1. Isaac and _____ are having a sleepover party.

2. They watch a movie and eat _____.

3. Isaac wants to play a _____ game.

4. Isaac wins the _____ game.

5. Julian's parents will wake up if the boys are not _____.

Balloon Surprise

Noah's sister is turning four years old. She loves balloons. Noah wants to surprise her with lots and lots of them. He spends the whole morning in his bedroom. His sister doesn't know what he is doing. He is blowing up balloons! Noah opens the bag of small balloons. He wants to give her as many balloons as he can. He wonders if he can fill his room with them. He might run out of breath first! It takes less than a minute to blow up each one. Soon he has twenty small balloons. But he needs big balloons, too. He opens the bag of bigger balloons. He blows some up. Then Noah starts blowing up a pink balloon. It looks like the biggest bubblegum bubble ever! He keeps blowing and blowing. Pop! The balloon couldn't get that big. Did his sister hear the balloon pop? Then Noah sees her through the window. She looks sad. Wait until she sees her birthday surprise! Noah ties all the balloons together with string.

Answer the questions below.

1. Who is having a birthday? _____

2. Where is Noah blowing up balloons? _____

3. What size balloons does he blow up first? _____

4. What happens when he makes a balloon too big? _____

_____

5. How does Noah keep the balloons together? _____

_____

Tree House

Zoe's uncle made a tree house for Zoe! It has a floor, a roof, and four walls. There are little windows and a door, too. Zoe loves being there. How does Zoe get to the tree house? Zoe's uncle made a wooden ladder. Zoe is safe when she goes up and down. Once her brother wanted to jump down instead. Zoe told him no. But he still jumped. He broke his leg! Zoe doesn't allow him in the tree house anymore. It is for girls only. Zoe invites Molly there almost every day. Molly is her best friend. They have secret meetings in the tree house. They talk about school and friends. Then they play house. Sometimes they eat snacks like sugar cookies or apples. They laugh and have fun. When it gets dark outside, it's time to come down from the tree house. Zoe and Molly use the wooden ladder. They never fall.

Read each sentence. Circle *true* or *false*.

1. Zoe loves her tree house.   true   false

2. Once she fell out and broke her leg.   true   false

3. Zoe and Molly have secret meetings in the tree house.   true   false

4. Sometimes they eat snacks.   true   false

5. When it gets dark, the girls keep playing.   true   false

Baking Bread

You can bake your own bread! First, get a very large bowl. Pour in a cup and a half of water. Add a little bit of honey, oil, and salt. Then empty a packet of yeast into the bowl. Pour three cups of bread flour into the bowl, too. Now stir it all well! This is the dough. But it's not ready to be baked. First, you must make the dough softer. You do this by kneading it. Kneading is pushing, turning, and folding the dough. Put some flour on your hands. Then they won't stick to the dough. Start kneading! You can stop when the dough is a ball. It should be as soft as your ear lobe. Then the dough must rest in the bowl. Cover it with a towel. Don't peek! The dough is rising because of the yeast. The yeast fills the dough with little air bubbles. This will make the bread chewy. Finally, the dough is ready for baking. Put it in a bread pan. Have an adult place the pan in the hot oven. The dough will need to bake for almost an hour. And then you will have your own warm bread!

Read each question. Circle the right answer.

1. Which item is not a part of bread dough?
   a. honey
   b. water
   c. sugar

2. How do you make the dough soft?
   a. Stir it.
   b. Knead it.
   c. Bounce it.

3. Where does the dough rise?
   a. in the oven
   b. in the bowl
   c. in the refrigerator

4. What happens if you forget the yeast?
   a. The dough will not rise.
   b. The dough will get hard.
   c. The dough will stay cold.

5. About how long should the bread bake?
   a. almost a minute
   b. almost an hour
   c. almost a day

Careful in the Kitchen

Hunter makes a ham sandwich for lunch. He wants to cut it in half. Mom opens a drawer. She uses a knife to cut his sandwich. She says the knives need to be kept in a safe place. Kids can hurt themselves with them. There are many other dangers in the kitchen. But there are easy ways to avoid getting hurt by them. She points to the locked cupboard under the sink. That is where she keeps the cleaners. They are poisonous! Kids could try to drink the cleaners. They might spill them on their skin. So she keeps them locked away. There are other dangers, too. Pots on the stove are very hot. It is easy to get burned. Mom always faces the pot handles in. That way no one will bump into them. She also watches food that is cooking. She must make sure that the food doesn't catch on fire. Another common danger in the kitchen is water on the floor. It is easy for anyone to slip on a spill. How can you avoid it? Just wipe up water right away!

Draw a line from each danger to a way to avoid getting hurt.

knives	Wipe up spills right away.
cleaners	Keep them in a drawer.
pot handles	Turn them in.
fire	Keep them in a locked cupboard.
water on floor	Watch food that is cooking.

At the Ocean

Kathryn's parents are taking her to the beach today. Kathryn has never been swimming in the ocean! At first, she is a little frightened. She stands at the edge. A tiny wave goes over her feet. She feels the sand pull away. But soon Kathryn is brave enough to go further. Now she is up to her waist. She sticks her head under the water. "Ew!" The water is so salty. She will keep her mouth closed! Then Kathryn swims a little. She rides the waves back to shore. The ocean is more fun than a pool! But then she feels something on her foot. She screams. She raises her foot and sees some green seaweed. Maybe it's time for a break. Kathryn dries herself with a towel. What happened to her hands? They are wrinkled. They look like raisins! It's because she was in the water too long. Then Kathryn walks along the edge of the ocean. Her feet leave marks in the sand. They disappear when the next wave comes. Kathryn likes the ocean.

Finish each sentence.

1. Kathryn and her family are swimming in the _____.

2. She rides the _____ back to shore.

3. _____ is on her foot.

4. Too long in the water makes her fingers look like _____.

5. Kathryn's feet leave marks in the _____.

Answer Key

Answers to some of the pages may vary.

Page 4

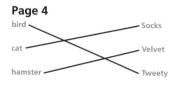

bird ——— Socks
cat ——— Velvet
hamster ——— Tweety

Page 5
1. a
2. b
3. c

Page 6
1. true
2. false
3. true

Page 7
1. ice
2. fish
3. eggs

Page 8
1. swing
2. Grace
3. pocket

Page 9
1. Mexico
2. guide
3. Maya

Page 10
1. c
2. a
3. c

Page 11
1. false
2. true
3. true

Page 12
1. pasta and meatballs
2. Ben
3. in the pot

Page 13
1. York
2. ferry
3. woman

Page 14
1. sunset
2. north
3. west

Page 15
1. b
2. a
3. c

Page 16
kids ——— cooking food
parents ——— rolling in grass
dogs ——— playing kickball

Page 17
1. true
2. false
3. false

Page 18
1. bowling
2. coat
3. ten

Page 19
1. machine
2. vanilla
3. snow

Page 20

first ——— Shelby buys balloons.
second ——— Shelby tells Dad that she wants ginger ale.
third ——— Shelby decorates the cake.

Page 21
1. c
2. b
3. a

Page 22
1. garden
2. knife
3. add dressing

Page 23
2 Bears sleep through the winter.
1 Bears make dens from leaves and small branches.
3 Bears and cubs wake up to eat.

Page 24
1. carnival
2. cuts
3. dinner

Page 25
first ——— The Sliders make a home run.
second ——— Ethan eats a hot dog.
third ——— Ethan and his dad find their seats.

Page 26
1. kites
2. tree
3. Marissa

Page 27
1. lightning
2. thunder
3. tree

Page 28
1. a
2. a
3. c

Page 29
2 Nicholas takes a shower.
3 Mom makes popcorn.
1 Nicholas's watch says 6:45.

Page 30
1. red apple
2. three
3. gums

Page 31
1. April
2. plant
3. reuse

Page 32
1. true
2. true
3. false

Page 33
1. Grandpa's house
2. He fell off his bike.
3. two months

Page 34
1. b
2. c
3. a
4. b

Page 35
1. false
2. true
3. false
4. true

Page 36
1. sleds
2. snow
3. legs
4. family

Page 37
1. a
2. c
3. a
4. b

Page 38
1. Texas
2. train
3. light shirts, shorts, and sandals
4. so she can sleep

Page 39
1. cotton
2. field
3. spin
4. weave

Page 40
1. computer
2. type
3. erase
4. copy

Page 41
1. true
2. false
3. true
4. false

Page 42
1. b
2. a
3. c
4. a

Page 43
1. pioneers
2. westward
3. wagons
4. farms

Page 44
1. José
2. animal shelter
3. black
4. in his arms

Page 45
1. guest
2. weekend
3. avocado
4. school

Page 46
1. a
2. b
3. b
4. a

Page 47
1. true
2. false
3. true
4. true

Page 48
1. desk
2. Maria
3. Carlos
4. writer

Page 49
1. tonight
2. blizzard
3. Dad
4. shovel

Page 50
1. oysters
2. pail
3. pearl
4. sand

Page 51
1. c
2. a
3. b
4. b

Page 52
1. false
2. false
3. true
4. true

Page 53
1. tigers
2. zoo
3. sleeping
4. bamboo

Page 54
1. Sasha
2. sprayed
3. odor
4. tomato

Page 55
1. fossils
2. bodies
3. dinosaurs
4. forests

Page 56
1. b
2. a
3. c
4. a

Page 57
1. false
2. true
3. false
4. true

Page 58
1. The butter melts.
2. Butter smears her report.
3. Paige doesn't receive a great grade.
4. Paige won't leave butter out again.

Page 59
1. read
2. He went blind.
3. Braille system
4. elevator buttons

Page 60
1. water
2. scared
3. Nate
4. nose

Page 61
1. lunch
2. banana
3. brown
4. lemon

Page 62
1. true
2. false
3. true
4. false

Page 63
1. b
2. a
3. c
4. b

Page 64
1. inside
2. Sophia
3. math
4. Luke
5. three

Page 65
1. money
2. She slipped and fell.
3. earrings
4. Gabby's mom
5. lucky

Page 66
1. baseball
2. play video games
3. ping-pong
4. He's tired.

Page 67
1. rays
2. summer
3. waterproof
4. hat
5. red

Page 68
1. false
2. false
3. false
4. false
5. true

Page 69
1. a
2. c
3. b
4. b
5. a

Page 70
1. karate
2. book
3. respect
4. belt
5. wait

Page 71
1. false
2. true
3. true
4. false
5. true

Page 72
1. before sunrise
2. lake
3. She puts worms on the hooks.
4. The fish is too strong.
5. bracelet

Page 73
1. July
2. fireworks
3. parade
4. our country
5. flag

Page 74
1. c
2. a
3. b
4. a
5. b

Page 75
1. research
2. public
3. magazines
4. borrow
5. card

Page 76
1. true
2. false
3. true
4. false
5. true

Page 77
1. hat shop
2. summer
3. cowboy hat
4. sun hat
5. It gets sweaty.

Page 78
1. a
2. c
3. b
4. c
5. b

Page 79
1. false
2. true
3. false
4. true
5. true

Page 80
1. day
2. elephants
3. tiger
4. stand
5. bikes

Page 81
1. ice
2. sport
3. swing
4. puck
5. point

Page 82
1. b
2. a
3. b
4. c
5. b

Page 83
1. fruit
2. woodpecker
3. one
4. acorns
5. roots

Page 84
1. false
2. true
3. false
4. true
5. false

Page 85
1. The car slows down.
2. Devin presses the gas pedal.
3. Devin stops the car.
4. The car turns.
5. Devin turns on the wipers.

Page 86
1. a
2. b
3. a
4. c
5. b

Page 87
1. hearing
2. inventor
3. thousand
4. music
5. light bulb

Page 88
1. Julian
2. popcorn
3. board
4. video
5. quiet

Page 89
1. Noah's sister
2. his bedroom
3. small
4. It pops.
5. He ties them with string.

Page 90
1. true
2. false
3. true
4. true
5. false

Page 91
1. c
2. b
3. b
4. a
5. b

Page 92

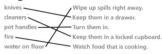

Page 93
1. ocean
2. waves
3. seaweed
4. raisins
5. sand